Rick Riordan

CHILDREN'S STORYTELLERS

by Christina Leaf

BLASTOFF! READERS 4

BELLWETHER MEDIA • MINNEAPOLIS, MN

Note to Librarians, Teachers, and Parents:

Blastoff! Readers are carefully developed by literacy experts and combine standards-based content with developmentally appropriate text.

Level 1 provides the most support through repetition of high-frequency words, light text, predictable sentence patterns, and strong visual support.

Level 2 offers early readers a bit more challenge through varied simple sentences, increased text load, and less repetition of high-frequency words.

Level 3 advances early-fluent readers toward fluency through increased text and concept load, less reliance on visuals, longer sentences, and more literary language.

Level 4 builds reading stamina by providing more text per page, increased use of punctuation, greater variation in sentence patterns, and increasingly challenging vocabulary.

Level 5 encourages children to move from "learning to read" to "reading to learn" by providing even more text, varied writing styles, and less familiar topics.

Whichever book is right for your reader, Blastoff! Readers are the perfect books to build confidence and encourage a love of reading that will last a lifetime!

This edition first published in 2016 by Bellwether Media, Inc.

No part of this publication may be reproduced in whole or in part without written permission of the publisher. For information regarding permission, write to Bellwether Media, Inc., Attention: Permissions Department, 5357 Penn Avenue South, Minneapolis, MN 55419.

Library of Congress Cataloging-in-Publication Data

Leaf, Christina.
  Rick Riordan / by Christina Leaf.
    pages cm. – (Blastoff! Readers. Children's Storytellers)
  Summary: "Simple text and full-color photographs introduce readers to Rick Riordan. Developed by literacy experts for students in second through fifth grade"– Provided by publisher.
  Includes bibliographical references and index.
  ISBN 978-1-62617-342-2 (hardcover : alk. paper)
  1. Riordan, Rick–Juvenile literature. 2. Authors, American–20th century–Biography–Juvenile literature. 3. Children's literature–Authorship–Juvenile literature. I. Title.
  PS3568.I5866Z76 2016
  813'.54–dc23
  [B]
                                   2015028671

Printed in the United States of America, North Mankato, MN.

Table of Contents

Who Is Rick Riordan?

Rick Riordan is the best-selling author of the Percy Jackson books and The Kane **Chronicles**. His modern **mythology** has made kids excited about stories from long ago.

Rick's **series** have turned many **reluctant** readers into book lovers. His books show that reading does not have to be boring. It can be an action-packed adventure!

A Reluctant Reader

Rick was born on June 5, 1964, in San Antonio, Texas. He was the only child of two teachers.

N
W   E
S

🏠 San Antonio, Texas

"I want to create a book that works for all kids, not just the big readers."
Rick Riordan

In school, Rick was not a great student. He had trouble paying attention and thought reading was boring. He preferred building things and playing with Legos.

"You have to find a story not just that you think it would be cool to write, but that sort of grabs you and says, 'oh, you have to write me.'"

Rick Riordan

In middle school, Rick read The Lord of the Rings series. He loved it! Then a teacher taught him about the **Norse** mythology in the books.

The ancient myths excited him. They sparked Rick's interest in writing. He even wrote **fantasy** stories he tried to **publish** in magazines.

Heroic Work

After college, Rick taught middle school English. His goal was to get kids excited about reading. Mythology was always a hit with his students.

Rick continued to write outside of work. His first book, *Big Red Tequila*, was published in 1997. It was the first book in a mystery series for adults.

fun fact

Rick also wrote *The Maze of Bones*. This is the first book in The 39 Clues series. Many different authors have written books for this series.

"I think kids want the same thing from a book that adults want — a fast-paced story, characters worth caring about, humor, surprises, and mystery."

Rick Riordan

At night, Rick told stories to his son, Haley. Rick wanted to keep him interested in school. Haley struggled with **ADHD** and **dyslexia**. He did not like reading. However, he enjoyed mythology.

Haley

! fun fact

Rick gave the first draft of *The Lightning Thief* to some of his students to read. They gave him tips on how to improve the story.

One night, Rick ran out of myths. He made up a new story about a hero named Percy Jackson. This became the first **draft** of *The Lightning Thief*.

Lightning Strikes

The *Lightning Thief* was published in 2005. At first, sales were slow. But soon, kids all over were reading about Percy and his friends.

SELECTED WORKS

Percy Jackson and the Olympians series (2005-2009)

The Maze of Bones **(from The 39 Clues series) (2008)**

The Heroes of Olympus series (2010-2014)

The Kane Chronicles (2010-2012)

Magnus Chase and the Gods of Asgard series (2015-)

Rick completed the series with four more books. Then he wrote about other mythologies. So far, he has written about Greek, Egyptian, Roman, and Norse myths!

Modern Myths

Rick's books for young readers are popular because they are exciting and funny. The magic and action of the stories keep kids turning pages. Modern-day settings place heroes and gods into the reader's world.

Narrators in middle school help readers **relate** to Rick's stories. The characters speak in ways kids understand. They make jokes and use slang words.

Rick's characters are stuck between the mythological and **mortal** worlds. Many readers can relate to feeling confused about where they belong.

Some of Rick's characters also have trouble in school. Percy has ADHD and dyslexia. However, these are skills in the hero world. This teaches kids that **learning disorders** may hide other strengths.

19

A Return to Olympus?

Rick does not plan to write any more books for his first three series. But the Magnus Chase series about Norse gods is not finished. He has also written short stories that combine characters from different series.

"Everything you could possibly want in a story is in Greek mythology."
Rick Riordan

IMPORTANT DATES

1964: Rick is born on June 5 in San Antonio, Texas.

1978: Rick submits his first story to a magazine.

1997: Rick's first book, *Big Red Tequila*, is published for adults.

2005: *The Lightning Thief*, the first Percy Jackson book, hits shelves.

2008: *The Maze of Bones*, the first book in The 39 Clues series, is published.

2010: *The Red Pyramid* is named one of the Best Books of the Year by *School Library Journal*.

2010: *The Lightning Thief* movie opens in theaters.

2011: Rick is named Author of the Year at the Children's Choice Book Awards.

2013: "The Son of Sobek," Rick's first short story with both Percy Jackson and Carter Kane, is released.

2015: *The Sword of Summer*, the first book in the Magnus Chase and the Gods of Asgard series, is published.

Rick says he has not left Percy's world for good. He may still return with new series to bring readers back to Mount Olympus.

Glossary

ADHD—a condition that makes it difficult for a person to focus and sit still; ADHD stands for attention deficit/hyperactivity disorder.

chronicles—stories of events in the order in which they happened

draft—a version of something made before the final version

dyslexia—a condition that makes it hard for a person to read, write, and spell

fantasy—a story set in an unreal world often with superhuman characters and monsters

learning disorders—conditions that affect how people understand, remember, and respond to new information

mortal—able to die; humans are often called mortals in mythology.

mythology—tales of the gods, half-gods, and heroes of a culture or a group of people

narrators—the characters who tell a story

Norse—from ancient Denmark, Norway, Sweden, or Iceland

publish—to print work for a public audience

relate—to connect with and understand

reluctant—unwilling to do something

series—numbers of things that are connected in a certain order

To Learn More

AT THE LIBRARY

Corbett, Sue. *Rick Riordan*. New York, N.Y.:
Marshall Cavendish Benchmark, 2013.

Riordan, Rick. *The Lightning Thief*. New York, N.Y.:
Miramax Books/ Hyperion Books for Children,
2005.

Wheeler, Jill C. *Rick Riordan*. Minneapolis, Minn.:
Abdo Pub. Co., 2013.

ON THE WEB

Learning more about Rick Riordan
is as easy as 1, 2, 3.

1. Go to www.factsurfer.com.

2. Enter "Rick Riordan" into the search box.

3. Click the "Surf" button and you will see a list of
   related web sites.

With factsurfer.com, finding more information is just
a click away.

Index

The images in this book are reproduced through the courtesy of: Janette Pellegrini/ Stringer/ Getty Images, front cover (left), p. 20; Yeng Moua, front cover (right); JLC/ ZOJ WENN Photos/ Newscom, p. 4; Sarah Kerver/ Stringer/ Getty Images, pp. 5, 6, 18; Amy Sussman/ Stringer/ Getty Images, pp. 7, 13, 16, 17; Taylor Hill/ Getty Images, p. 8; Domini Brown, pp. 9, 15, 21; Bob Hallinen/ MCT/ Newscom, p. 11; Johnny Louis/ JL/ Sipa USA/ Newscom, p. 12; ZUMA Press/ Alamy, p. 14; Mary Evans Picture Library/ Age Fotostock, p. 19.